AF344836

Minnows Coasting Downstream

the poetry of
ayaz daryl nielsen

Copyright© 2023 ayaz daryl nielsen
ISBN: 978-93-90601-84-4

First Edition: 2023
Rs. 200/-

Cyberwit.net
HIG 45 Kaushambi Kunj, Kalindipuram
Allahabad - 211011 (U.P.) India
http://www.cyberwit.net
Tel: +(91) 9415091004
E-mail: info@cyberwit.net

No part of this book may be reproduced or transmitted in any form or by
any means, electronic, mechanical, photocopying, or otherwise, without
the express written consent of ayaz daryl nielsen.

for Judith

ayaz daryl nielsen, veteran and hospice/home health nurse, lives in Longmont, Colorado, USA. Editor of *bear creek haiku* (35+ years/ 165+ issues) with poetry published worldwide, he is online at: *bear creek haiku   poetry, poems and info*.

Among other deeply appreciated honors, he is especially delighted by the depth and heart of poets worldwide whose poems have a home in *bear creek haiku's* print and online presence.

welcome emptiness
the truth needs no furniture
it simply just is

your detailed letters
steadfastly engaged in a
poets ways of life

numinous daybreak
looking around carefully
everything as is

yea, sure

ornery cuss
living next to us
claims to be
a 'realized'
student of
Buddhism

unknown photograph
stiff with yearning hopefulness
hanging from a nail

alongside the road
as I replace the flat tire
crow cawing darkness

a laundry closet
expressed my opposition
stomped out the wrong door

nearby balcony
the lady in red velvet
blowing kisses

everything
the secret name
of anything

even if you were a
velveteen angel
couldn't love you more
than I already do

everything has been
everything will be
within numinous emptiness
everything
becomes us

mother nature
recycling, too, the
beautiful roses

Minnows Coasting Downstream

fireflies   a forgotten dream
working on haiku
while slowly strolling
along the sidewalk…
soon, nose-to-brick
in dead-end alley

and words take my hand
pushing me from narrowness
stating "we're ready"

black and white magpie
robins flitting through garden
no emptiness here

the world just keeps
on turning toward
the bright side
and may we, yes,
the many of us
also keep on
turning toward light

every blade of grass
faith, fear, grit, wind, love and loss
seeing and being

esoteric studies while
seated at my shrine
outside the window
two crows chuckling
poetic license
this very small pond
one fervent frog

a hazy sunset
moving across the blue sky
how much more is there?

these willow branches
dabbling in a quiet stream
butterflies hovering

beside an elm tree

Autumn leaves, as they
fall from their elm branches
shake, shimmer, quiver…
I find myself
practicing new
dance moves

hang 'em high

her undies, my undies
on the same clothesline
swinging, dreaming
together
as one

assumed my wife
was sound asleep
as I farted
quickly
learned otherwise

after speaking
as I leave the podium
the young man's smirk

every
solitary
teardrop

even
just
one

naked

as we dance,
dear one,
with nothing on
but love

carved from our heartland
this soft stirring of moments
finding their way home

fragrance of pinecones
the moon women's reflections
dancing among trees

late night embraces
shadows sway in bright moonlight
their caring whispers

and this golden tan
wandering through life's stories
all the hidden suns

cities of mountains
how long they have been around
templates of the real

perhaps a new mirror
this one reflects
last year's fool

twilight flickers
among the saguaro
moonbeams or chindé?

spring, come soon
grandpa again insists his
tractor is restless

homeless elder
crumpled
cardboard sign
the corner of
Alpine and 9th…
I miss him

leaves crackle underfoot
baskets of apples and plums
stacks of grains and years

setting aside
the holy books
a long walk
among fireflies
under stars

this path lined with
bristlecone and juniper
dreaming of home

a vase with red
and yellow roses
upon the glossy
mahogany table
a petal, falling

in our searching for
the thin grip of certainty
this uncertainty
buttercup blossoms
choosing their sunlit angles
seeking the poetic

ancestors and descendants
always
every moment

in its full splendor
a meadow full of daisies
alongside the path

a verdant garden
the garden scarecrow and I
watching each other

of all things human
those of us just plain confused
pause- - look- - start!, again- -

and here it is, my life,
reduced to four lines
and I still, so often,
get it wrong

morning, again,
everywhere
the now of us
yield to it
marbled within all
6,000 and some
of our languages
the concept of love

rising from my meditations
with questions and answers
one and the same

our six-year-old
granddaughter,
blurting, "I need
a change of
bun-derwear!"

at the funeral
writing a poem as
the casket descends

life insurance salesman
in the alley
dead

returning
my heart knows
the way

today, again,
our dog shit
on the grouchy
neighbor's
front yard- -
and yes, today,
again, I'll just
leave it there

much more beautiful
than any alone
us, as one,
unfurling

the mind's landscapes
therein one often
seeks, and finds,
welcome release

our days, yes,
our days, together
a oneness of us
the oneness of us

yes, there is
this grief—
and a new
morning's
rising sun

a social presence
the translucent poetic
within creating

"hon, I'm here to stay"
that day in early summer
luggage tossed aside

exhausted, jealous
over the ocean
people soundly sleeping
I can't swim that far

journey continues
wandering among mountains
their diamond moments

my horses hooves
drumbeats beneath birdsong
an eagle rises

these streaming moments
eternity's pounding current
the eagle rises

like a child's drawing
an evening's radiant sun
these colorful hues
peace within our home
irrevocable choices
thankful for this life

no fruit nor veggies
open ground once the garden
an empire of weeds

crystal chandeliers
earth's spell-bound celebrations
wild-flowers opening

Minnows Coasting Downstream

nation-wide tremors
loved ones sitting together
our own fresh portrait

without known words
truth lifted out of silence
it's own element

let's hope so

a flag, so faded
so sun-bleached
could be anyone's
could be everyone's

skidding on the ice
toward the wrong side of the road
and my car breaks free

drifting on this lake
farther and further away
from shoreline and angst

far across the field
widening and approaching
a golden raincloud

having gone further
than I ever have before
much further to go

poetics
surrounding our adult lives
the gardens within

these tranquil seasons
our embrace of human life
evenings together

wind from a mountain
autumn's yellow aspen leaves
floating down the stream

miles of frozen ice
as we glide across the lake
pause and rub noses

and such a rainbow
as it arches over us
the brief cathedral

winter's twilight sky
evening stars shine through a cloud
as if listening

these waves come and go
a sense of one's confidence
as waves come and go

a soundless darkness
the shadows between houses
as they settle in

fading twilight sky
as if going somewhere else
beyond the darkness

beloved hobby
printing presses still whirling
poetry's ballast

basking in sunlight
mushrooms and the wild-flowers
earth's emissaries

land-locked in dry dock
it's future undecided
the rusty tugboat

as a dark shadow
seeping into late night sleep
yesterday's turmoil

these days come and go
nights pass ever so quickly
I love you, darling

kitty up a tree
all the birds have flown away
kitty can't get down

kitty near a tree
noisy crow above splatters
poop upon her head

leathery full moon
or is it that I've just seen
so many sunsets

these seismic tremors
collapsing infrastructures
the earth's own crusade

early morning walk
 soft reminiscence within
  this gossamer mist

the canyon's echo's
no response when I'm yelling
a nasty cuss word

upon the shelving
in the hero's library
all, with our own book

campfires last embers
gathering our camping gear
we choose to move on

all lights are turned off
as I look through a window
alley-cat looks back

across this meadow
an ocean of wildflowers
meadowlarks trilling

bottomless pail
as we pick wild blueberries
eating most of them

of all things themselves
out of such life consciousness
poet's flowing pen

this sudden Spring wind
holding her skirt down, mumbling,
"didn't wear undies"

beautiful landscapes
lilacs and honey suckle
poet's flowing pen

her open coffin
flowers on a nearby stand
suddenly bloom

uncle's bison ranch
buffalo still unwilling
to cross railroad tracks

arms and legs tattooed
first date with his future wife
she has a few, too

turning the light out
a fiery shooting star streaks
through the dark night sky

mashed squirrel on the road
other squirrels noisy mourning
from nearby branches

a brilliant rainbow
suddenly appears over
my road most traveled

muddy to my knees
should have taken my pants off
but no underwear

wading in bear creek
squishy mud between my toes
last days of summer

rain and warm weather
from these many lily pads
horny chanting toads

midnight on the lake
strumming guitars in the boat
wasted and happy

washing potatoes
the tub has a subtle leak
my pants look peed in

thick haze to the west
smoke from the forest fires
can't see the mountains

pauses between noise
it's as if this lovely day
waits with quiet hugs

on this big 'ole nose
the one hair I didn't shave
glistens in sunlight

outside on this day
warmth and thoughts of grandparents
their hugs still linger

the 4th of July
my biggest aerial firework
sails through a window

neighbor and close friend
his dear wife just passed away
come, we'll take a walk

grumble, grumble
ice cold and slippery slush
my big pair of winter boots
talking to each other

a fading rainbow
replaced by the rising moon
now how cool is that

wind from the mountains
our Lakota neighbor says
"Spirit of the land"

in the midst of work
longing for wild greenery
days of private calm

each and all moments
eternity's presence thrums
through human lifelines

the wail of bagpipes
on this blistery hot day
an eagle rises

the waves come and go
this sense of self-confidence
waves come and waves go
dreaming

middle of the night
death measuring my lifeline
shorter than I hoped

quite the enigma
those who are seeking refuge
falsely imprisoned

passing through the mist
a mist that doesn't notice
glimmers of eagle

your lips softly
seeking upon mine
your arms around
my shoulders
mine around yours
the cathedral of us

murmurs in hallway
something gentle about them
friends enter the room

"too soon, dry and extinct"
you mean, the weather, she asks
no, I mean myself

slowly and with joy
walking among wet snowflakes
damp nose, silly grin

an august morning
sunlight across rumpled bedding
the cat is snoring
sure, I'm told, blame the cat

those past acid trips
impossible to forget
couldn't find 'I am'

sitting quietly
in the study
time for long
overdue
conversations
with house plants

4:15's ennui
one more hour
to 4:30

minnows
coasting downstream

that's all!

www.ingramcontent.com/pod-product-compliance
Lightning Source LLC
LaVergne TN
LVHW041803190726
843493LV00008B/2775